On It, Phonics! Vowel Sounds

The Ant Is Black

The Short A Sound

By Connor Stratton

level 1

little blue readers

www.littlebluehousebooks.com

Little Blue House is distributed by North Star Editions:
sales@northstareditions.com | 888-417-0195

Produced for Little Blue House by Red Line Editorial.

Reading Consultant: Andrew P. Johnson, PhD, Distinguished Faculty Scholar and Professor of Literacy Instruction, Minnesota State University, Mankato

Photographs ©: iStockphoto, cover; Shutterstock Images, 5 (ant), 5 (bat), 5 (cat), 5 (fan), 5 (hat), 5 (mat), 5 (pan), 5 (rat), 5 (van), 6, 9, 11, 13, 15, 17, 19, 21, 23

Library of Congress Control Number: 2023909721

ISBN
978-1-64619-919-8 (hardcover)
978-1-64619-937-2 (paperback)
978-1-64619-972-3 (ebook pdf)
978-1-64619-955-6 (hosted ebook)

Printed in the United States of America
Mankato, MN
102023

About the Author

Connor Stratton writes and edits nonfiction children's books. He lives in Minnesota.

Table of Contents

Consultant Note

"On It, Phonics!" is designed to reinforce vowel sounds, beginning blends, and sight words and to provide reading practice for young readers. Books like these are one important part of a comprehensive literacy program for students at emergent and beginning levels. "On It, Phonics!" should be used with other high-quality children's books. Instructors and parents are advised to go over the words in the picture glossary before students begin reading, and review the sight words after students finish reading. You can also ask students to go back and identify words with the target letter-sound.

Andrew P. Johnson, PhD,
Distinguished Faculty Scholar and
Professor of Literacy Instruction,
Minnesota State University, Mankato

Short A Picture Glossary

ant

bat

cat

fan

hat

mat

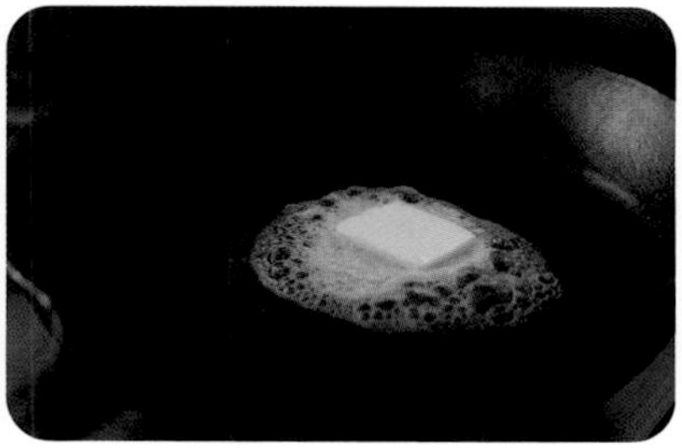

pan

rat

van

ant

Black

The ant is black.

The bat is black.

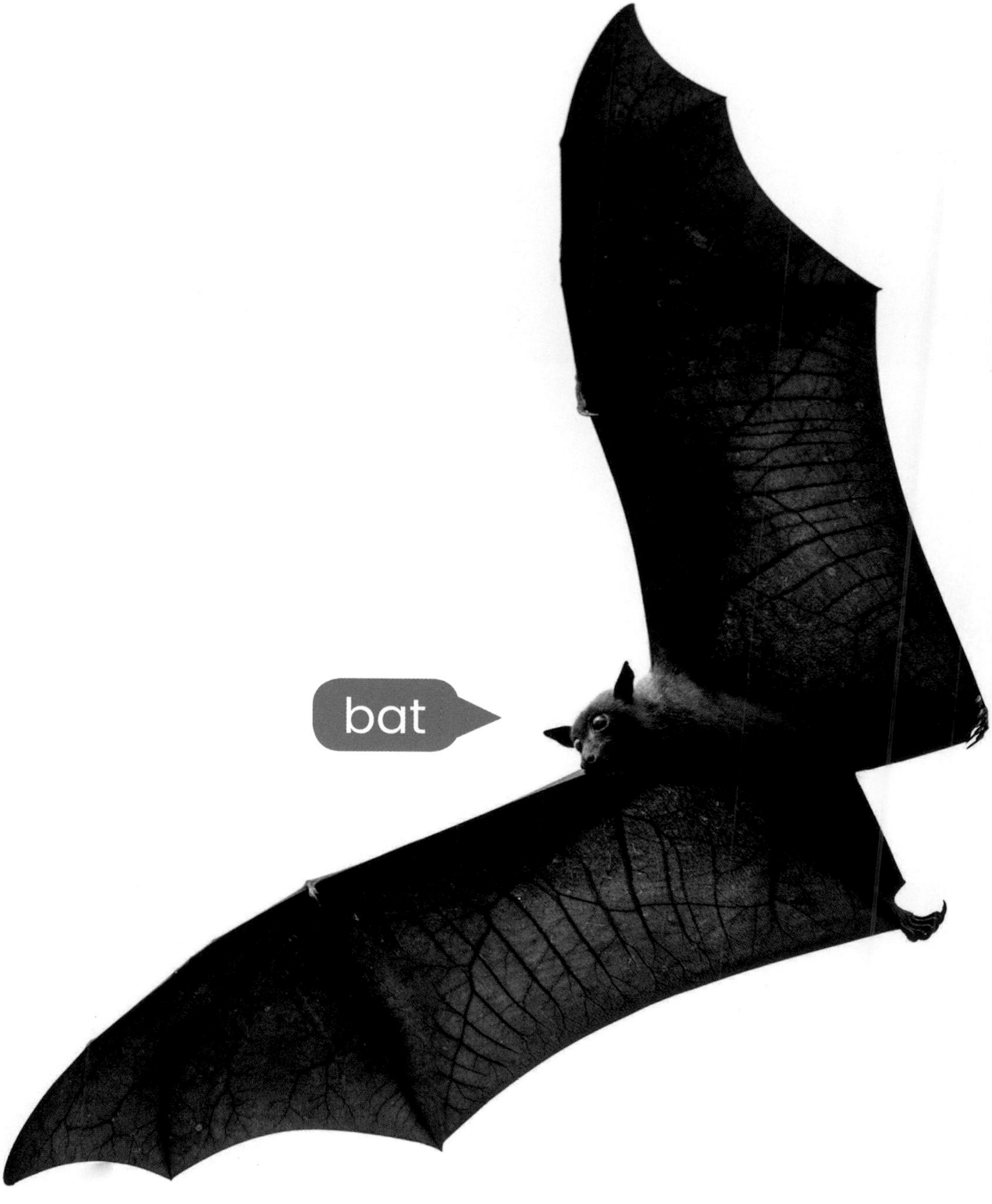
bat

The rat is black.

rat

The cat is black.

cat

The mat is black.

WOOF
mat

The hat is black.

hat

The fan is black.

fan

The pan is black.

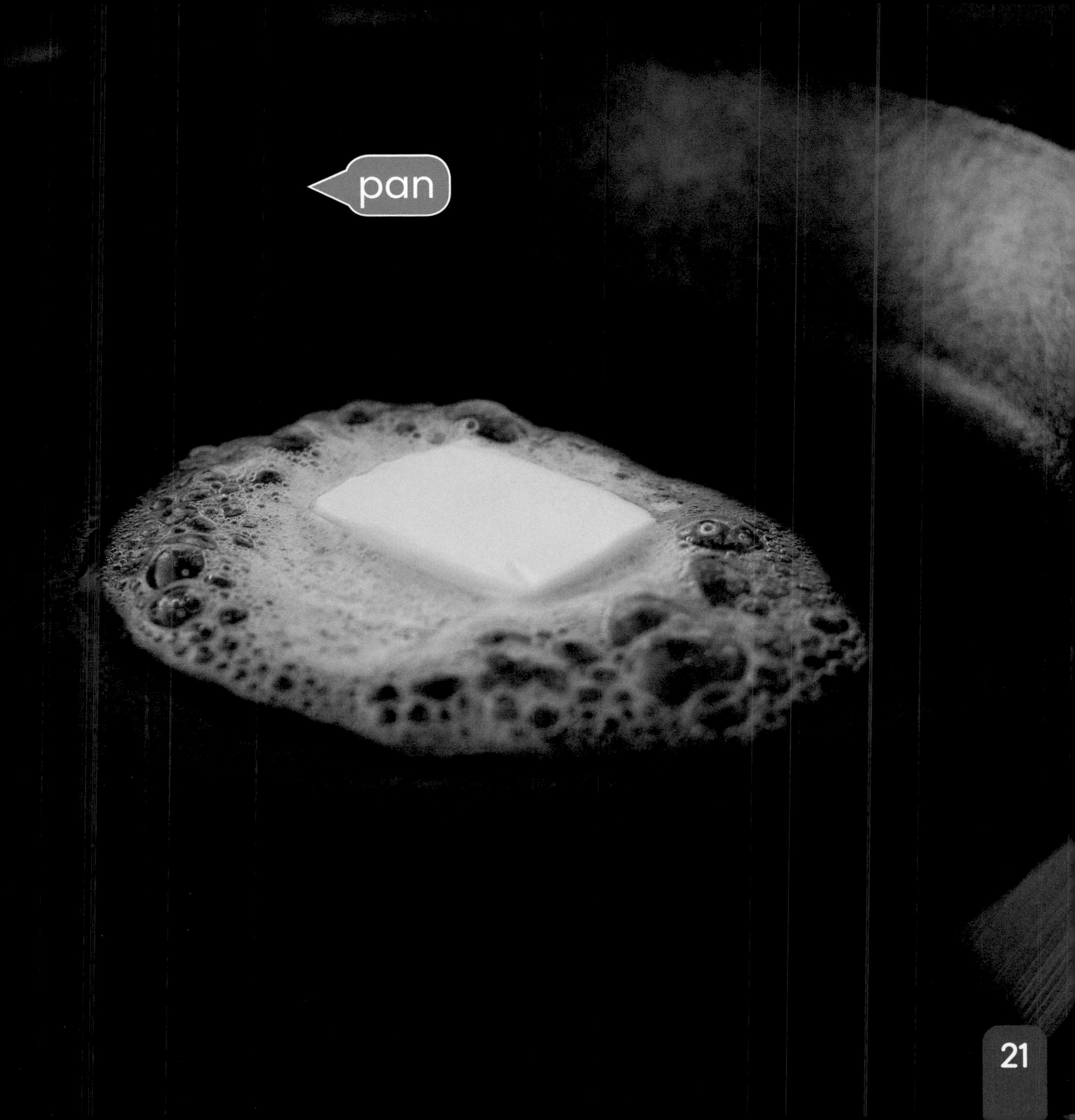
pan

The van is black.

van

Sight Words

black

is

the